The GRID DESIGN Workbook

CINDY SEITZ-KRUG

AQS Publishing

The American Quilter's Society or AQS is dedicated to quilting excellence. AQS promotes the triumphs of today's quilter, while remaining dedicated to the quilting tradition. We believe in the promotion of this art and craft through AQS Publishing and AQS QuiltWeek®.

Content Editor: Adriana Fitch
Graphic Design: Lynda Smith
Cover Design: Sarah Bozone
Quilt Photography: Charles R. Lynch,
How-to-Photos: Cindy Seitz-Krug
Proof Reader: Chrystal Abhalter
Director of Publications: Kimberly Holland Tetrev

Additional copies of this book may be ordered from the American Quilter's Society, PO Box 3290, Paducah, KY 42002-3290, or online at www.ShopAQS.com.

Text and design © 2016, Cindy Seitz-Krug
Artwork © 2016, American Quilter's Society

American Quilter's Society
www.AmericanQuilter.com

**Library of Congress
Cataloging-in-Publication Data**

Names: Seitz-Krug, Cindy, author.
Title: The grid design workbook / by Cindy Seitz-Krug.
Description: Paducah, KY : American Quilter's Society, 2016.
Identifiers: LCCN 2016043604 (print) | LCCN 2016044159 (ebook) | ISBN
  9781683390114 (pbk.) | ISBN 9781683395126 (ebook)
Subjects: LCSH: Machine quilting--Patterns. | Quilting--Patterns. | Grids
  (Crisscross patterns)
Classification: LCC TT835 .S444 2016 (print) | LCC TT835 (ebook) | DDC
  746.46/041--dc23
LC record available at https://lccn.loc.gov/2016043604

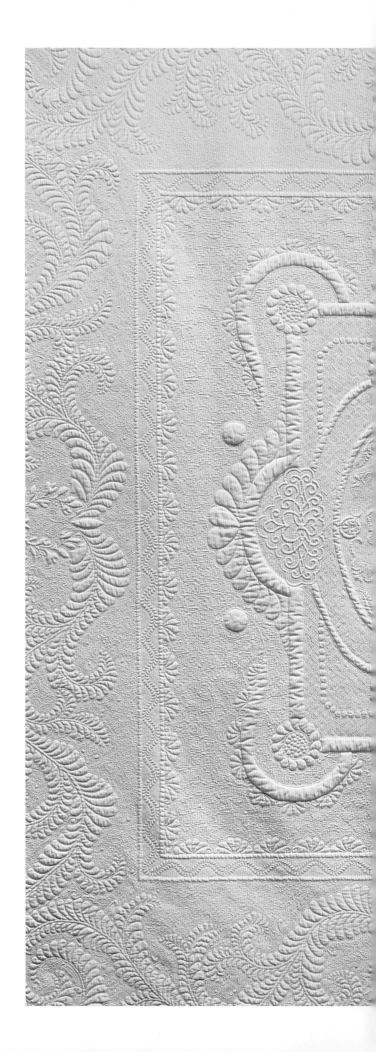

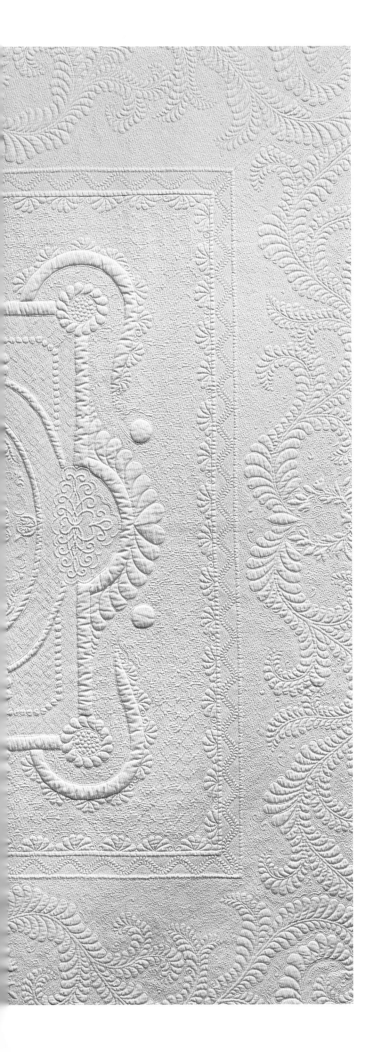

Acknowledgments

I am happy to have this opportunity to thank the heirloom quilters who have come before me and dazzled thousands of quilters with their beautiful quilting. First of all, thank you, Diane Gaudynski, for being the biggest influence in my quilting life. To this day, I am awestruck whenever I see your work. If it weren't for you, I would not be the quilter that I am. Your never-ending kindness and generosity are infinitely appreciated. I also wish to thank Cindy Needham for her beautiful heirloom quilting on antique linens. Her quilting is exquisite, and I am continually amazed at her willingness to openly share her "trade secrets" with all of us. Last, I'd like to extend a special "thank you" to Harriet Hargrave for starting the machine quilting revolution. It's hard to imagine life before machine quilting.

I am thrilled to see all of the new and upcoming quilters that have taken heirloom quilting to the next level and continue to amaze all of us with their innovative quilting designs. As with the rapid advancement we see in technology, the same rapid evolution appears to be happening with quilting. It is phenomenal to see all of the fabulous quilting on every manner of quilt. It's so exciting to attend a quilt show or look online and see the amazing quilting that's being done today. So all you quilters, past and present, please continue to dazzle all of us! You may not know it, but you are inspiring a new generation of quilters.

Dedication

I dedicate this book to my mother, Anita Seitz. I've always known how fortunate I am to have her as my mother. All my life she's set the perfect example for me with her honesty, integrity, work ethic, and unconditional love. Thank you, Mom! I love you!

P.S. Thanks, too, for signing me up for my first quilting class.

Table of Contents

Introduction:
Grid-Based Designs All Around Us

Grid-based designs are all around us. In fact, they're so common that you probably don't even realize what you're seeing when you see one, but the fact is, your eye is drawn to it. When you walk into a home décor shop or look through magazines with decorating ideas, you are probably staring at one gridded design, if not several.

What about grid-based designs in quilts? Whether you're looking at a book filled with quilts from the last decade or several hundred years ago, your eye is drawn to the beauty of gridded designs.

Why do we love these designs so much? It's my guess that our brains like their structure and symmetry. What really makes them so appealing is that they help to enhance the fancier designs (whether in home décor or in quilting) to which they are a backdrop. Their simple elegance makes the things around them shine even more, in a synergistic manner.

Gridded designs take a bit longer to execute because the base grid has to be marked onto the quilt first, and sometimes that same grid has to be sewn before the "design" can be stitched. So these designs take longer, but the result is oh so worth it!

This book was written to teach the reader how to quilt many beautiful gridded designs to make the other aspects of their quilts shine even more. I quilt on a home sewing machine, but these designs can be quilted on a longarm quilting machine just as easily.

I hope you enjoy the photos in this book that demonstrate the beauty of gridded quilting designs. Once you look through this book, your eyes will be opened to all the gridded designs around us and you'll be inspired to incorporate them into your quilts.

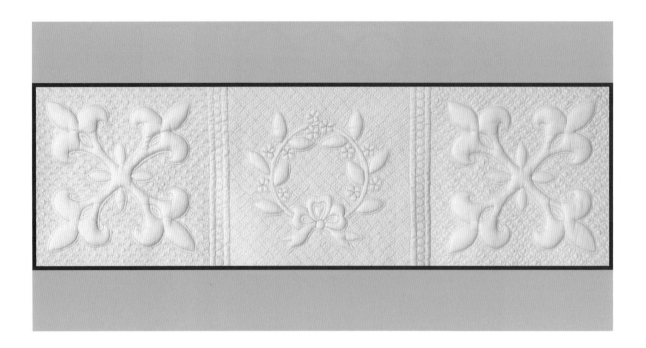

Chapter 1:
Getting Started

Now that your quilt top is finished and you've decided that you'd like to incorporate a grid-based design into the quilting, you need to think about the following things: marking your quilt top, choosing your thread(s), and pin basting the quilt.

Marking the Grids

The first thing you need to decide is which type of marking tool you would like to use. I have two favorite marking pens. To mark light-colored fabrics, I use a blue water-soluble marker by Clover. I prefer to use the type with a thick tip (the fine tips tend to drag on fabric and marks don't show up as well as the thick tips). If you use one of these pens to mark your quilt top, be sure that it is a new or relatively new pen. If it's old and dried up, the marks won't show up well enough for you to see them and you may have to re-mark some of the lines. Be careful when using these blue markers to never subject them to heat. When you wash your quilt to remove the marks, use only cold clear water—not hot or warm water. You never want to iron on top of these blue marks. You also shouldn't leave your marked quilt in a hot car or in direct sunlight, as the marks can set in and turn brown.

If your quilt top fabric is dark, you may want to use the fine white marking pen by Clover. This pen looks like a gel pen, and when you start marking your quilting designs with it, you may think it's not working because it takes about 30 seconds for the marks to show up. But I find that it works very well on solid-colored dark fabrics. (It does not show up well on medium or printed fabrics). To remove these white marks, the package says to just "iron them out." Well, ironing does make them disappear, but they're really not gone. They can reappear in cold water or cold temperatures. To completely remove the marks, I wash the quilt in warm water. If I still see white marks after the quilt has dried, I use a burst of steam from my iron to completely get rid of them.

Clover® water-soluble markers: blue for light fabrics and white for dark

Before you pin baste your quilt for machine quilting, it is best to mark the entire quilt. This takes a bit of pre-planning of your quilting designs, but it is much easier to mark a quilt top that doesn't have batting under it or safety pins to get in your way. Your grid marks will also be much more accurate.

You can choose several different options when it comes to marking your background grid. Here are a few tools to choose from:

Ruler: You can simply use a ruler to mark your grids if that's all you have. This technique can be very accurate if you take the time to mark each line consistently, but it can be tedious, too. It's not my favorite method to mark grids.

Stencils: There are many types of grid stencils on the market today. The only drawback to these is that the "intersections" in the grid may have to be marked in by hand later (depending on the grid design), and this is a bit of extra work, but necessary for successful grid quilting.

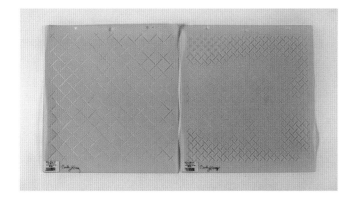

Left: 1" diagonal grid   Right: ½" diagonal grid

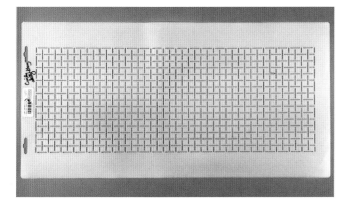

½" horizontal/vertical grid

Another great tool for marking your background grid is the June Tailor® Grid Marker™ tool. This tool has continuous lines that are ½" apart. This means that if you want to mark a 1" grid, you just skip every other line. Or, if you want a ¼" grid, you mark your ½" lines, then move the template ¼" so that you can mark another set of lines in between the ½" lines. To use this tool, you would mark all your vertical lines first, and then your horizontal lines next. Since the lines are continuous, there's no need to go back and draw in the intersections, which is a big plus. The only drawback to this tool is that it is fairly small in size, so you have to move it often to cover larger areas of your quilt.

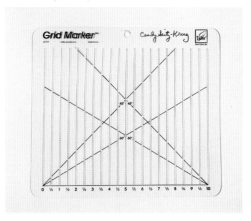

Pin Basting

My preferred method of basting a quilt is with safety pins. Machine quilters don't normally hand baste their quilts with thread, because if you quilt over the thread, you'll have to pick that thread out later with a seam ripper.

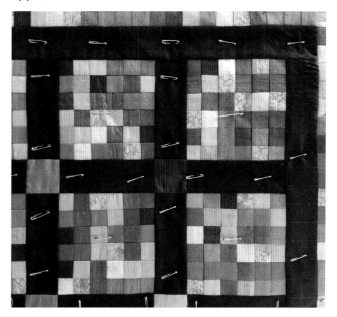

Safety pins are set approximately 4" apart.

Choosing Thread

Without question, you need to use a very fine thread to do this type of intricate background quilting.* If you use a thread that is 50-wt or larger, your designs won't look elegant and graceful; they could look clunky and too "thready." Also, your mistakes will be MUCH MORE NOTICEABLE!

My favorite thread to use for background grid designs is 100-wt. silk thread (Kimono Silk by Superior Threads or YLI Silk #100 thread). However, there are many other fine threads on the market that could work just as well, such as a lightweight cotton or a pretty polyester.

*If you're using these grid-based designs on patchwork rather than as a background fill, heavier threads are fine and will show up well.

Something you should always keep in mind for this type of quilting is that whatever you choose to use for your top thread should also be used in the bobbin (or at least something that is a VERY close match in weight and color). Even the best quilters will sometimes see their bobbin thread pop up to the top of the quilt, even with a nearly perfect tension setting. So to avoid this, use matching thread.

I would also suggest that unless you're an extremely confident quilter, you should use a thread color that closely matches your fabric, or just a shade lighter. Thread that is darker than your fabric (even slightly darker) will show mistakes much more than you'd probably like.

Also remember that when using fine threads such as those mentioned above, you should use a size 70/10 needle or possibly even a 60/8 needle. My two favorite quilting needles are titanium topstitch needles by Superior or Schmetz Microtex Sharp needles.

Tricks for Success

Before you start quilting your background grid designs, ALWAYS add a row of echo quilting around your main quilt motif (whether it be appliqué or a plain quilting design). For this row of echo quilting, be sure to use the same thread that you'll be using for stitching your background grid design. This row of echo quilting will serve as your pathway for traveling when you're quilting your background designs. If you do not add that row of echo quilting, you'll have to lock off your threads every time you come to the main motif; or, you'll have to travel along the motif itself, which won't look good if you have two different threads.

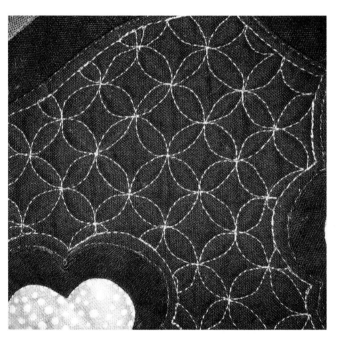

Note the row of echo quilting next to the black appliqué, using pink thread.

Because I used the same color thread for the echo quilting and the background grid design, I was able to use the row of echo quilting to travel, when necessary.

If I had not echo quilted around the appliqué, I would have had to travel next to the appliqué, and that would have looked horrible with pink thread.

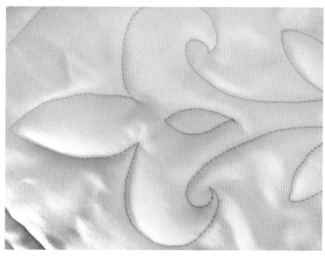

Quilt motif without a row of echo quilting

Quilt motif with echo quilting

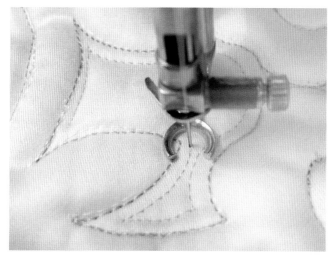

Adding the row of echo quilting with the same thread to be used for the background quilting design

Please remember this one thing as you start; YOU ARE NOT A MACHINE! Do not expect your stitches to be as perfect as they would be if you were programming them into a computer to stitch out. It won't be perfect by any means, but if you take your time and strive for accuracy, you'll create beautiful designs.

Chapter 2:
Clamshell

Clamshell designs go back hundreds of years and can often be seen in quilting designs, fabric prints, and home décor accents, such as wallpaper. They are also prevalent in Sashiko quilting designs.

Clamshell designs are one of the easiest gridded designs to quilt, because you don't have to stitch the base grid lines. Just use those lines as your guides for the Clamshell pattern.

Procedure:

1. Mark a horizontal/vertical grid on your quilt. It is not mandatory to connect the intersections with your pen for this design.

2. Starting at an intersection, make an arc up to the intersection above and to the right. When you touch that point, make another arc down to the next intersection to the right. You will end up with a row of half circles that are two blocks wide on your grid.

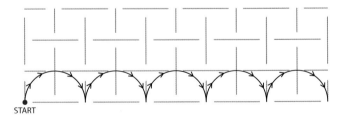

<table>
<tr><td>TIP
I find it easiest to work from the bottom of the grid upward.</td></tr>
</table>

3. When you reach the end of your row or space, travel up to the next row and head back the other way (left). This time your half circles will end each time in the exact center of the half circle below it.

START

TRAVEL
LINES

TIP
Take your time with this design and try to hit
the center of the half circle below each time.

An open-toe free-motion foot allows for better visibility when aiming for the center point of the Clamshell below.

Clamshell pattern on 1" patchwork block

Clamshell variations:

Actual size of Clamshells:

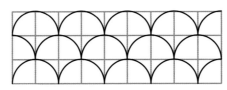

¼" Grid

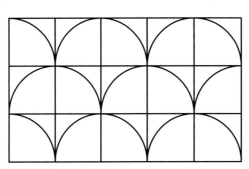

½" Grid

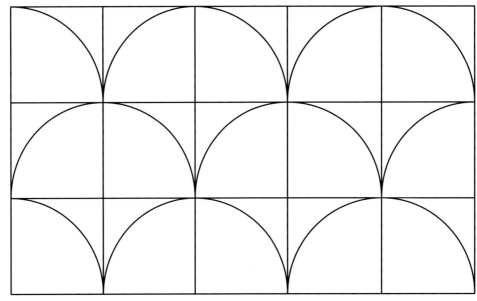

1" Grid

Chapter 3:
Cathedral Window & Orange Peel

The Cathedral Window quilting design is named so because it looks just like a patchwork Cathedral Window pattern. Whenever I see this quilting design used on a quilt, my eye is always drawn to it, and I can't help but admire the inherent beauty of the pattern. I see this same reaction with so many other quilters. When something is that beautiful, it is definitely worth the time it takes to learn the stitch and how to perfect it.

Detail of Cathedral Window pattern in quilting

Procedure:

1. Mark your grid. You can decide whether you want to mark a horizontal/vertical grid or a diagonal grid.

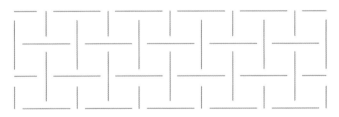

2. Stitch all grid lines (you may choose to use your walking foot, or a free-motion technique, including ruler foot and ¼" ruler).

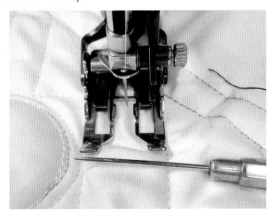

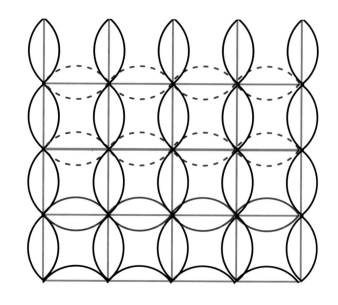

3. Choose one of the following options for quilting the curves:

Option 1: "Soft S" method

Start at an intersection of the base grid and stitch out a bit from the grid line. When you get to the middle of that grid line section, curve back in toward the next intersection (you've stitch an arc). Next, stitch onto the other side of the grid line and repeat. You will be stitching a "Soft S" shape from grid block to grid block, with half of the "S" in one block and the other half of the "S" in the adjoining block. When you get to the end of the grid line, stitch back down the same grid line. Once you finish this line, stitch over to the next grid line and repeat.

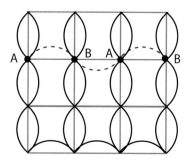

Looking from point A to point B, visualize a circle. Then complete that circle with stitches.

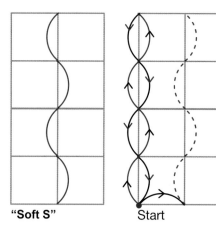

"Soft S"   Start

Once you have completed all of the curved lines going in one direction, you will start to stitch the curved lines going the other direction (i.e., once you've finished your vertical curved lines, then you'll be ready to stitch your horizontal curved lines).

Option 2: "Continuous-Curve" method

Start at an intersection and stitch out slightly from the grid line. At the middle of the grid line, curve back in toward the next intersection, making an arc. Do not cross the intersection. Follow the 1 2 3 pattern as shown below:

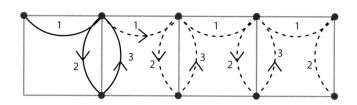

When you reach the end of a row, stitch a series of arcs across the bottom of the grid blocks to complete that row of your design.

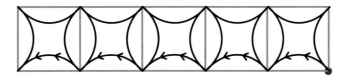

Repeat for all rows.

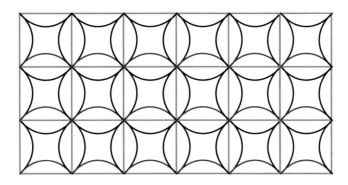

> **TIP**
> Be careful with this method, because it is harder
> to make your intersections meet precisely.

The Orange Peel design is identical to the Cathedral Window design except that it does not have the grid lines sewn in. Therefore, you get a very different look.

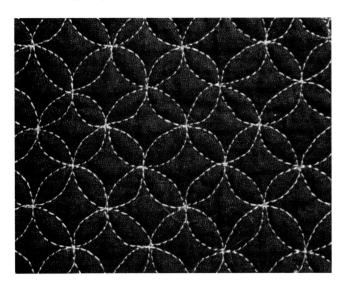

There is an additional step in this design that will make quilting it easier, and that is that you should first draw in your "intersections" on your grid (if your grid stencil doesn't have connecting intersections).

Instructions for quilting the Orange Peel design are the same as for the Cathedral Window. As with the Cathedral Window, the Orange Peel looks wonderful whether quilted on a diagonal grid or a horizontal/vertical grid.

Cathedral Window and Orange Peel quilting used in patchwork

Actual size of Orange Peels and Cathedral Windows
½" Grid

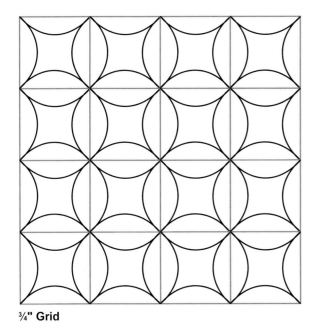

¾" Grid

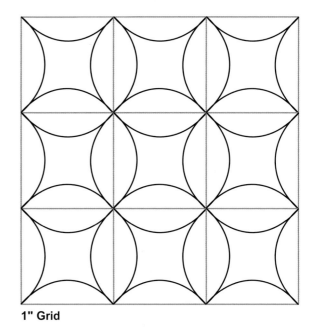

1" Grid

Additional Options

Chapter 4:
Basket Weave

The Basket Weave design is one that we see often, whether it's used in cake decorating, knitting patterns, tile work, or home décor. Its simplicity is one of the reasons it is so beautiful and popular, and if you can count to five, you can easily learn to quilt this stitch.

Procedure:

1. Decide what size grid will work best for your quilt. Then decide whether you want the design to be horizontal/vertical or on the "diagonal." Once those decisions are made, mark your grid.

TIP
Start at a corner and work toward the other end of your space. For this block-shaped design, you want to show the full pattern in the corners and along edges, if possible. If you get to the opposite end of your space and only have ½ of a space, you might want to think about "fudging" your grid a bit to eliminate that extra space.

The Basket Weave pattern started in the corner (grey) shows a full square design.

Look at the following photos to see several scenarios when planning your grid markings for the Basket Weave.

This ½" grid fits perfectly on this appliqué block. Therefore, no need to "fudge" or compensate for partial grid spaces.

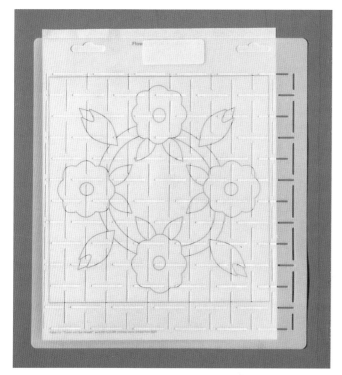

This ¾" grid doesn't fit the block perfectly, so some "fudging" is required.

By moving the grid stencil a bit, I was able to avoid having my partial grid spaces be so noticeable.

I realize that making your grid fit isn't all that important to some people. If it doesn't bother you to have a partial pattern at the edge of your space, then don't worry about trying to make things fit. Just mark away and be happy! But if you're very particular about things being perfect, then the above photos should help you to make your designs fit the space better.

2. Prepare to stitch. It is not necessary to connect the intersections of your grid for this design, nor do you have to sew the grid lines.

Starting in a corner, stitch along one line of the grid until you come to a perpendicular grid line. When you get to that perpendicular grid line, stop stitching and pivot (i.e., change direction of stitching). Stitch along the perpendicular grid line about two stitches if you are using ½" grid. If you have a 1" grid, stitch about four stitches. Switch directions (i.e., pivot) and go back the other direction, stitching parallel to the first line. We will count this line of stitching as #2. These two lines will be about ⅛" apart on a ½" grid. When you get to the grid line that is perpendicular to this line, switch directions again (make a 90-degree turn) and stitch over about two stitches, then switch directions and repeat the process. This will be the #3 line, and should be approximately in the center of that grid block. Repeat the process again for line #4, and then line #5, which will be along the marked grid line.

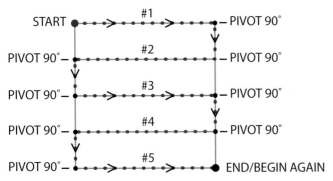

3. After you've completed one block in your grid (five parallel lines), you will make a 90-degree turn into the next block of your grid. You will repeat the same process that you performed in the first block, but these five lines will be the opposite direction from the first block. In other words, if the five lines in block 1 were all horizontal, then the five lines in block 2 will be vertical. For every block in the grid, the direction of the five parallel lines will alternate back and forth.

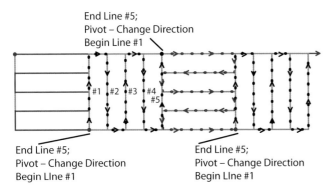

When stitching this design, it's important to count the five lines each time, because you know when you finish the fifth line, you have to change directions and start counting with 1 again.

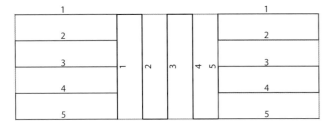

4. When stitching this design, take your time and be sure to make your corners (direction changes) square. This looks much better than sewing your lines in an "S" manner. Making "S" patterns is a nice design, but it doesn't really look like a Basket Weave.

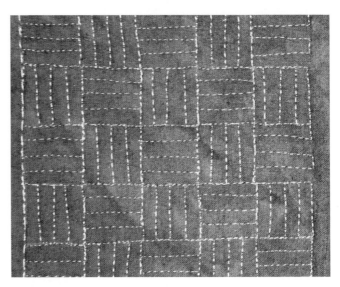

Top: correct manner of stitching
Bottom: "S" pattern doesn't look like a Basket Weave

Never do one section of your quilt, and then move over to another section and try to work back toward the section of Basket Weave you've already completed. If you do this, you have a 50% chance of meeting up with the previously stitched area and having your grid blocks going the wrong way.

In the next diagram, I started stitching in the top-left corner of the block (orange). But, I got bored with this and decided to change things up a bit and move down to the right-hand corner (purple). But when my Basket Weave patterns met up, I had a BIG PROBLEM. Where they met, the "weave" was going the same direction. There is no way to fix this except to remove your stitching.

Start 1: Stitching from left to right
Start 2: Stitching from right to left, then up the left side

Kitty corner blocks on your design will always have Basket Weave lines going in the same direction. Noting this helps to keep your stitching in the proper direction.

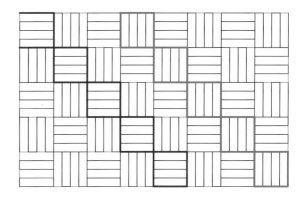

5. If you feel a pucker starting to happen (too much fullness in the area you're quilting), stop and stick a few extra safety pins in that area to redistribute the fullness. Using a lot of safety pins for this design is highly recommended because it's such a dense stitch.

6. If you get off track (i.e., two squares in your grid have lines going in the same direction), STOP! You must stop and rip out the stitches that are going the wrong way. This problem will not fix itself by ignoring it! You have to stop and make the correction. Just remember, when you get to the end of line 5, always switch directions.

This is what happens if you forget to pivot after counting five lines. This problem will not "self-correct." You must stop and remove the stitching that is incorrect.

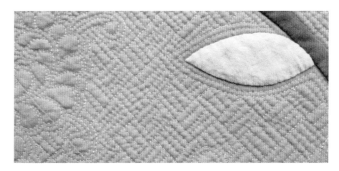

SIMPLY SANTA FE detail; made by author. Beautiful Basket Weave quilting shown as a background for appliqué and feathered quilting motif.

Actual sizes of Basket Weave

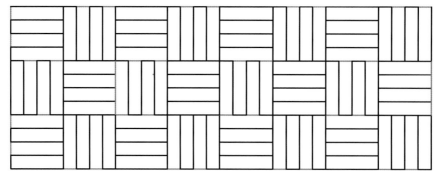

½" Grid

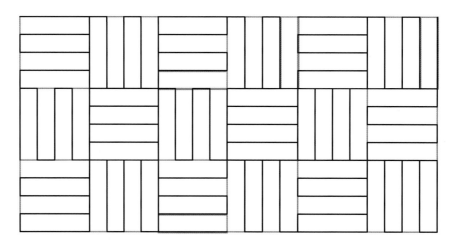

¾" Grid

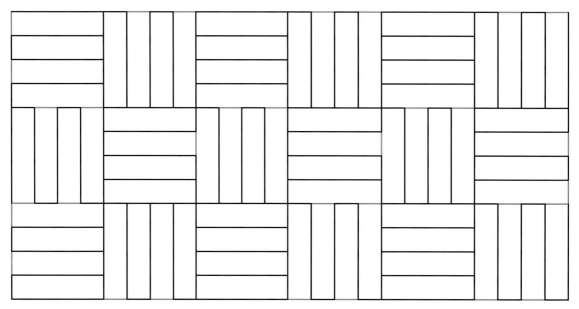

1" Grid

Chapter 5:
Optical Illusions

For lack of a better name, I've just called these next two stitches my Optical Illusion designs. Both of these designs are the same stitch, but for the first pattern shown in this chapter, all of the blocks in the grid are filled in the same direction. For the other design variation, half the blocks are filled one way (i.e., up/down), and the other half of the grid blocks are filled the other way (i.e., left/right). These two stitches are really fun and easy, and I know you'll enjoy using them in your quilts!

When all fillers go in the same direction it creates a design simply because the "negative space" (un-quilted area) puffs up so that the grid itself is what you mainly see.

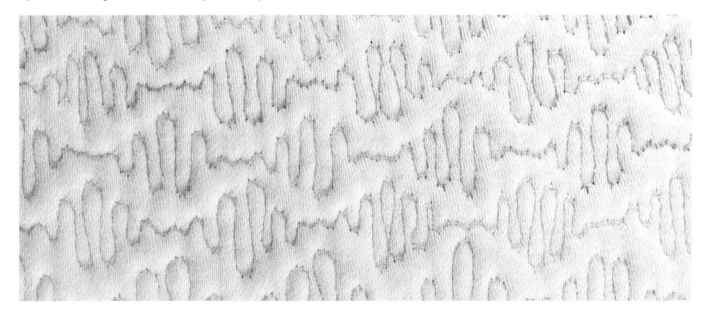

When the fillers go in the opposite directions, they create a completely different design.

Procedure for Optical Illusion #1:

1. Mark a diagonal grid on your quilt. (This design must be on the diagonal for it to work.)

It is not necessary for you to connect the intersections on your marked grid.

2. Starting at a corner, start filling a diagonal gridded square in an elongated "S" pattern. After you've filled that square, just cross over the intersection into the next square and repeat the process, all the way to the end of your quilting area.

START

YES

NO

Quilt in rows or columns and leave about ⅛" space between stitching and grid line.

Matching thread color allows you to see the "puff" more and the thread less.

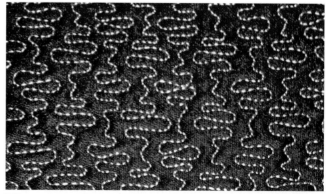

When you use colored thread, you don't see the "puff."

Procedure for Optical Illusion #2:

1. Mark the grid on the diagonal. Again, use a ¾" or 1" grid. No need to connect intersections.

2. Start in a corner and fill one row of squares up and down (as in the previous design). However, two things will change for this design. First, you should take your "S" shape stitches all the way to your marked grid line. Second, when you reach the end of one row, skip one row before starting back down with your "S" shapes. So, every other row will be quilted for now.

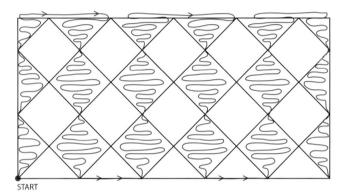

START

Note how the "S" shapes touch the grid lines.

3. Once every other row is filled with your up/down "S" designs, you're ready to start filling in the open squares. Quilt the remaining squares in a left/right direction rather than up/down. This will create an entirely different optical illusion when you've finished your quilting.

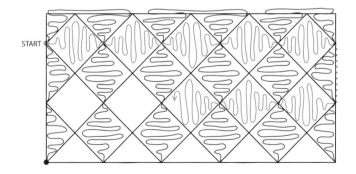

START

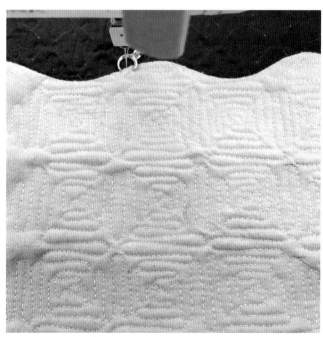

Filling in remaining grid blocks in the opposite direction creates a completely different design.

Actual size of Optical Illusions

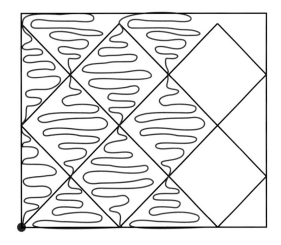 

¾" Grid actual size of design(s)

1" Grid actual size of design(s)

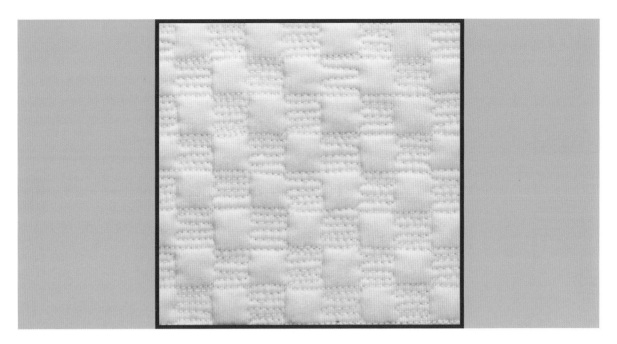

Chapter 6:
Checkerboard

The Checkerboard design is quite striking to look at, and it works extremely well in pieced quilts because of its geometric design. I especially like to use it on sashings and narrow borders. Another wonderful aspect to this design is that it quilts up very quickly.

Procedure:

1. Draw your grid. It is not necessary to connect the intersections for this design. Make sure that you can see your grid marks well because you'll need to have good visibility when you start filling in the grid squares.

TIP

Base the size of your grid (½", ¾", 1") on the size of the space you're filling. For example, if you have a 1" sashing to quilt, a ½" grid will fit perfectly and you'll have 2 rows of checkers. You wouldn't want to use a ¾" grid because then you'd only have 1 row of checkers plus a partial row, which wouldn't look good. However, if you have a 1½" sashing or border, you could use either a ½" grid (3 rows of checkers), or a ¾" grid (2 rows of checkers).

---

2. Once your grid is marked, you're ready to start quilting. Pick a corner to start. I usually start at the lower left-hand corner and work up, but it really is a personal choice and doesn't matter.

For this design you will quilt two rows at a time. Fill in one square with parallel lines. Once that square is filled, travel all the way over to the second row and fill in the next square. When that square is filled, travel back to the left and fill in the next square in the first row. Continue doing this until you reach the top of your two rows.

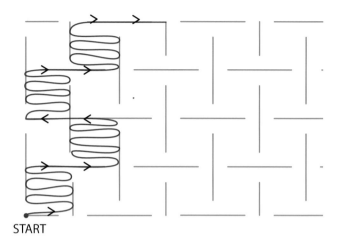

START

When you get to the top of those two rows, you will stitch over to start the next two rows (going the opposite direction which in this case is "down"). Note: The term "row" is used here for simplicity, but "column" would be the more accurate term.

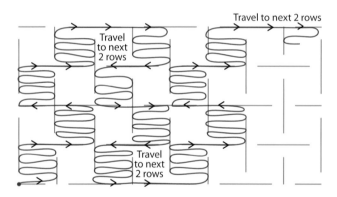

Travel to next 2 rows

Travel to next 2 rows

Travel to next 2 rows

Travel to next 2 rows

Checkerboard effect with matching thread

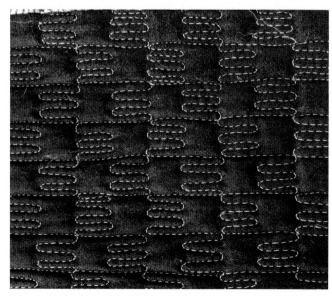

Checkerboard design with colored thread (you see the thread and not the checkerboard)

Actual Sizes of Checkerboards:

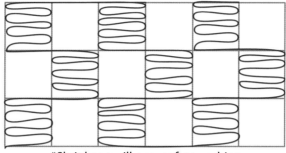

*Shrinkage will occur after washing,
so finished design will be smaller

½" Grid

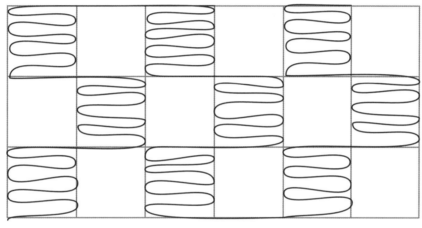

¾" Grid

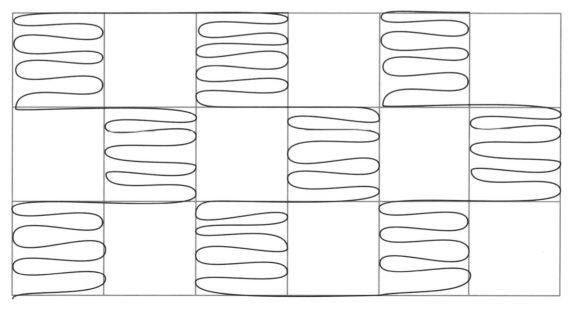

1" Grid

Chapter 7:
Square in a Square

The Square-in-a-Square design is similar to the Basket Weave because you simply have to count to five in each block in order to stay on track. However, the Basket Weave had five horizontal/vertical parallel lines in each block of the grid that were equal in length; the Square-in-a-Square design has five unequal diagonal lines. This pattern is a bit more difficult to stitch out and requires some concentration, but it is worth the added effort.

Procedure:

1. Mark a horizontal/vertical grid and connect the intersections.

> **TIP**
> Be sure to try to center your grid stencil (or ruler lines) to fit your space well.

Notice how the grid is centered on the triangle. Planning your marking ahead like this will make the finished design look much better.

2. Add diagonal lines to your grid.

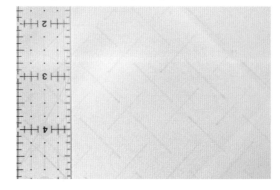

NOTE: Diagonal lines should ONLY be drawn in every other space as shown. Also Make sure your diagonal lines cross the intersections correctly.

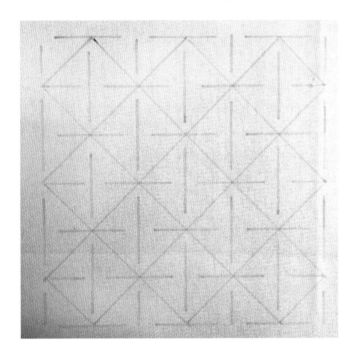

In the diagram shown below, this grid was marked in the following order:

1) Horizontal/Vertical grid was drawn first
2) Intersections were connected
3) Diagonal lines were added, making sure to skip every other horizontal or vertical line

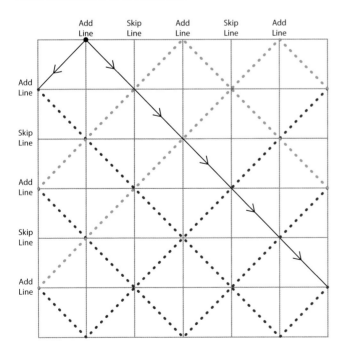

3. Starting about ⅓ of the way down from a corner in the grid, stitch a diagonal (45-degree) line up to the other corner of your grid square.

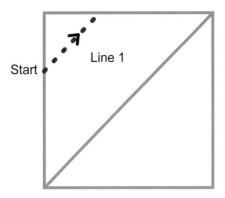

4. Travel over about ⅓ of the grid line to start your second line, stop, and pivot back in the opposite direction and stitch a parallel line next to the first line.

> **TIP**
> For this second line, it is helpful to "divide the space" between line #1 and the marked diagonal grid line that will be line #3.

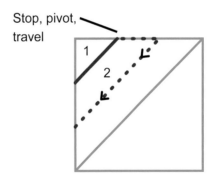

5. Once you reach the grid line, STOP, pivot, and travel down to the corner of the grid. At the corner, you'll start the third line. This one is easy because you just stitch on the diagonal grid line that is already marked.

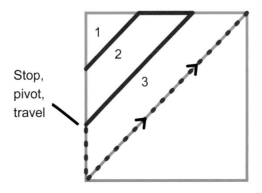

6. When you've reached the opposite corner with line #3, stop, pivot, and travel down the outer line of your grid block about ⅓ of the way down. Then pivot again and stitch a line parallel to line #3. This line will be your fourth line, and it will end on the bottom grid line about ⅓ of the way from the corner.

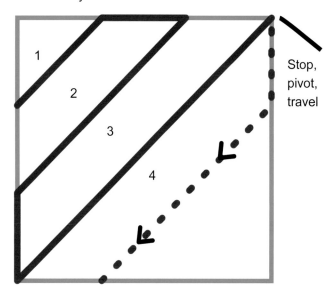

Stop, pivot, travel

7. Once you've completed line #4, stop, pivot, and travel to the right on the grid line about ⅓ more. Then stop, pivot, and stitch parallel to line #4 until you reach the marked grid line. That will complete line #5, and one entire block of this pattern.

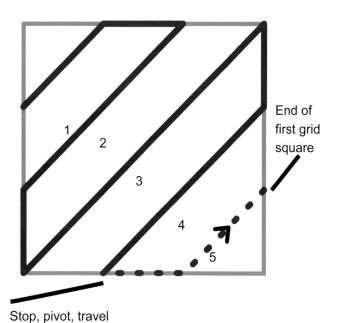

End of first grid square

Stop, pivot, travel

8. When you've finished a block, pivot 45 degrees and start another block in your grid with line #1. In this block, all your lines will be going the opposite direction from the lines in the first block.

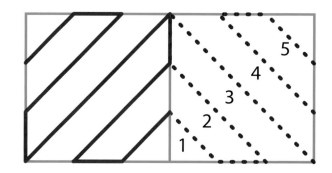

Finishing the 5 lines in one block and getting ready to pivot into the adjoining grid block. (Note: This is a 1" grid.)

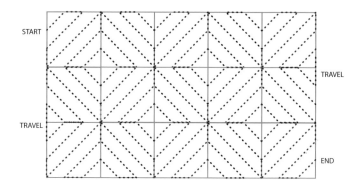

9. Once you've finished an entire row of your grid, travel down to the next row and work your way back. Your first and fifth lines in each grid block will join with the blocks adjoining them to form a small square in the center. The other lines will form squares around the inner square.

Tips for Success

First of all, REMEMBER THAT YOU ARE NOT A MACHINE! Your lines will not be perfectly straight, nor will they always line up with the other lines perfectly. Don't agonize over this. Just do your best and take your time. If you can do that, the result will be beautiful and unique.

Practice this stitch first. I recommend doing your practice on a 1" grid. This will allow you to see what you're doing so you can get a feel for the design.

When you start a new line of stitching, LOOK AHEAD TO WHERE YOU WANT TO END THAT LINE OF STITCHING. If you can look ahead to where you're going, you'll get there with a straighter, smoother line.

Actual sizes of Square in a Square:

½" Grid

¾" Grid

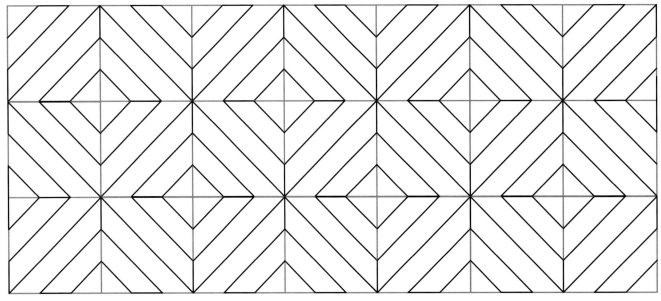

1" Grid

Chapter 8:
Greek Key

The Greek Key design originated in ancient Greece. It is also called "Meandros," after the Meander River, which is very twisty and doubles onto itself, giving a symbolic meaning to the key and the eternal flow of life.

Today we see Greek Key designs in many places. We see them in architecture, fabrics, stationery, and home décor. We also see them commonly used in quilts! However, we don't usually see them used as a background quilting design.

Procedure:

1. Mark your grid either on the horizontal/vertical axis or on the diagonal. It's a bit easier to quilt this design on the horizontal/vertical axis because you don't have triangles at the end of each row to contend with. It is optional whether you connect the intersections with your marking pen or not, but it could be helpful if you have trouble getting the hang of this design.

TIP

Until you become comfortable with the flow of this design, you might want to start with a 1" grid. The larger squares will allow you to see your pattern better.

MISSION ACCOMPLISHED (detail) by the author

2. I like to start this design in the bottom left-hand corner of my space. The first line of stitching goes straight up the blue line to the top of the grid square. Proceed to pivot to the right, again stitching on the blue line. Before getting to the next blue line (the right side of that grid square), stop about ⅛" short of the blue line, pivot, and stitch down.* Again, before reaching the bottom blue line, stop short, pivot, and stitch to the left, about ¼" from the blue grid line that marks the bottom of that square. Continue to fill the square as shown in the next diagram.

These instructions are written for stitching in a 1" grid.

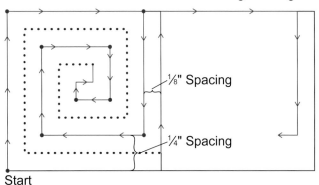

Start

→——→— Stitching lines going into the center

● Pivot points

• • • • • Exit of stitching. Notice how to divide the space

Key things to remember

1) The first two lines (and only these two lines) are stitched on the blue grid line.

2) The second line of stitching stops about ⅛" from the right side blue grid line. (⅛" is a relative term. It is correct for this 1" grid, but if you use a smaller grid, your estimated space will be smaller.)

3) The third line of stitching has to stop about ¼" from the bottom blue grid line because when you exit that square to move on to the adjoining square, you will "divide the space" between the fourth line and the blue marked grid line beneath it.

4) As you work in to the center of your grid block, keep your stitching lines approximately ¼" apart. This will allow you to neatly divide the space upon exiting with nice lines that are ⅛" apart.

Once you've completed one block in your grid, move on to the adjoining block and repeat the process.

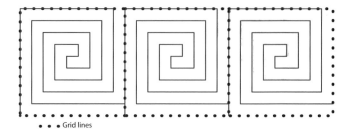

• • • Grid lines

3. When you get to the end of your row, travel upward and start working your way back in the other direction. If changing direction causes you to have heart failure, don't worry! You'll get the hang of it after a few practice tries. Just follow all the basic rules and your Greek Key design will turn out beautifully.

Travel up to next row

START

Line of stitching "exiting" the design, dividing the space

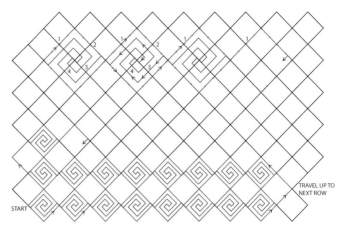

Finishing the area with Greek Key quilting

Variation:

This pattern skips every other row of diagonal squares in your grid. It works very well as a background fill, or as a simple border in a 1½" or smaller border or sashing.

It is stitched almost identically to the other Greek Key design except when you're filling in a square, you will stitch on every line of your grid that you're filling in. (Remember in our other design, we stitched lines 1 and 2 on the blue line, but left two lines to be stitched later when quilting an adjoining block.)

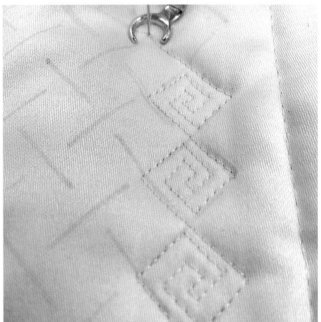

First row of Greek Key variation stitching

Filling a border with the Greek Key variation design

Greek Key quilting design used in 1" patchwork squares

Tips for Success

*Take your time and strive for straight lines and sharp corners.

*When you're working in toward the middle of the design, be planning your exit strategy. Remember when you exit, DIVIDE THE SPACE!

*Before you actually stitch this design, get out your 1" grid practice paper and practice drawing it.

Actual Sizes of the Greek Key

½" Grid

¾" Grid

1" Grid

Chapter 9:
Plover

The Plover design is commonly seen in Sashiko quilting. It is extremely versatile and enhances the overall interest and beauty of any quilt in which it is used. It's also beautiful no matter what size of grid is used. Best of all, it's easy to quilt!

Procedure:

1. Mark the desired size of grid on your quilt. I find it helpful to connect the intersections for better results when quilting this design.

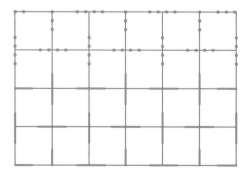

2. Once your grid is marked, pick a starting point for your stitching (usually a corner), and make a "soft S" shape along the grid line.

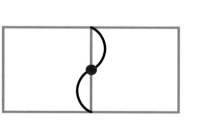
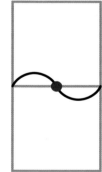

TIP
Strive to have your "S" cross the grid line in the center.

Travel through the intersection (try to hit that point with your stitching) and repeat that same Soft S shape all the way across your marked grid.

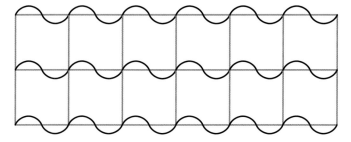

> ### TIP
> Be sure to stitch all of the grid lines that go in one direction first (either horizontal or vertical; either diagonal right or diagonal left). Make sure that all the lines are exactly parallel (i.e., soft S shape is the same direction in each grid block).

The first set of lines being stitched for the Plover design

3. Once you've finished stitching all the soft S lines in one direction, start stitching the same soft S pattern on the grid lines going in the other direction. Make sure that all of the shapes are identical, otherwise you'll create a totally different design.

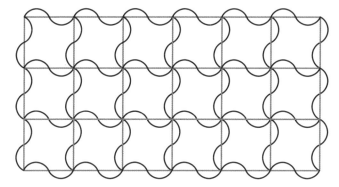

Below is a different design that is created if your S shapes are not identical each time.

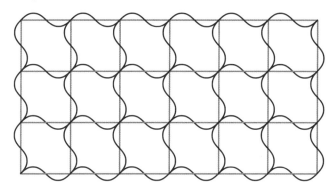

The S shape is stitched one way on the horizontal lines, but the mirror image of that S is used for the vertical lines.

Adding the second set of lines to create the Plover design

The Grid Design Workbook • Cindy Seitz-Krug • 41

Another Option: Diamond Gridded Plover design. (Diamond grid stencil purchased from www.cindyneedham.com)

Plover quilting on 1" patchwork

Actual Sizes of the Ploves:

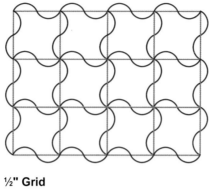

½" Grid

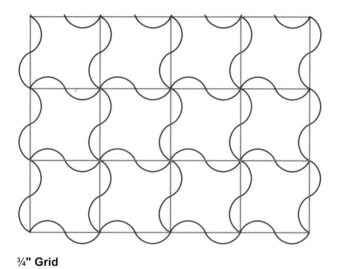

¾" Grid

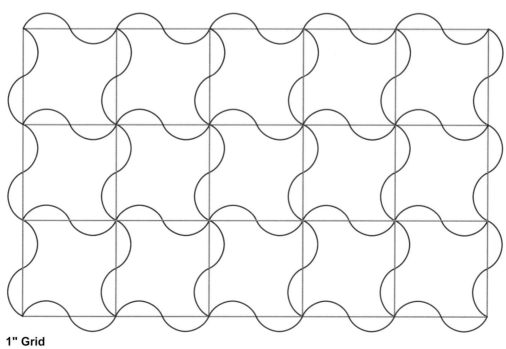

1" Grid

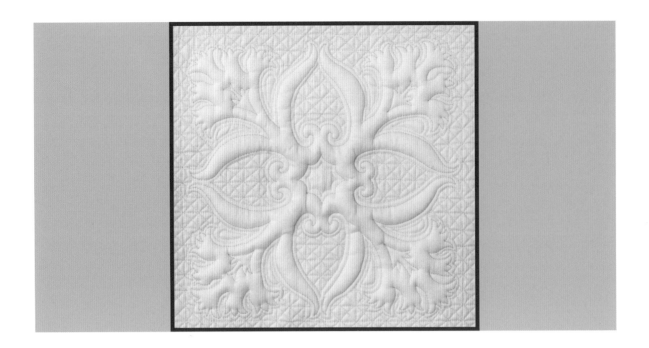

Chapter 10:
Double/Triple Grid

The Double/Triple Grid has a beautifully classic look. It works well in any situation in which you would use traditional crosshatching.

If using a walking foot to stitch these lines, it can be a somewhat slow and tedious process. However, with the advent of "ruler feet" and ¼" rulers for our domestic sewing machines, this stitch is now quick and easy!

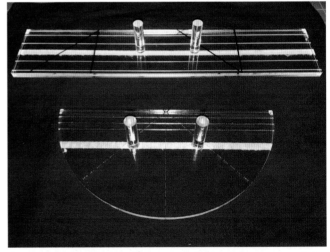

Quarter-inch thick rulers were formerly only used by longarm quilters, but are now being used by domestic machine quilters as well.

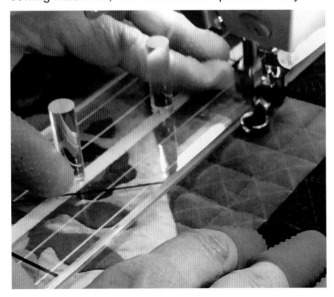

Quilting the Double/Triple Grid design with a ¼" ruler and ruler foot

Ruler foot with BERNINA adaptor to fit my sewing machine

Procedure:

1. First mark a 1" horizontal/vertical grid. Then, using a ruler, draw diagonal lines connecting the corners of the horizontal/vertical grid.

1" Horizontal/Vertical Grid

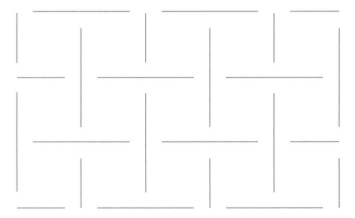

Add the diagonal lines, intersecting the points on the 1" grid.

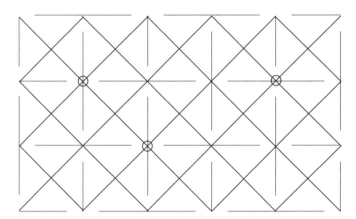

NOTE: The diagonal lines WILL NOT BE 1" apart. But they must connect at the intersections so that the design looks like it should.

Horizontal/Vertical 1" grid marked

Diagonal lines drawn, connecting the intersections of the 1" grid. The diagonal lines are NOT 1" apart.

2. Once you've marked your entire grid, simply stitch out the design on the marked lines. Again, the method of stitching is up to you. You may use your walking foot, free motion quilt with a ruler and ruler foot, or simply free motion quilt the pattern. The last option is least recommended though because it can be quite difficult, even for the best quilters, to get accurate, straight lines when free motion quilting.

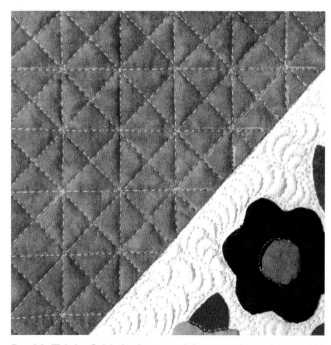

Double/Triple Grid design used in a setting triangle (1" grid)

Double/Triple grid quilting used in patchwork with 1" squares. The patchwork squares were quilted in the ditch first, and then the diagonal lines were added to complete the quilting design.

TIP

In my opinion, grids smaller than 1" get too small and too difficult to stitch out, so all the effort is wasted. I never go smaller than a 1" horizontal/vertical grid on my quilts.

Actual Sizes of Double/Triple Grids:

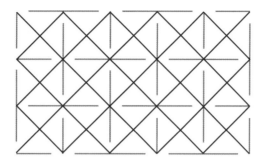

1/2" Horizontal/Vertical Grid

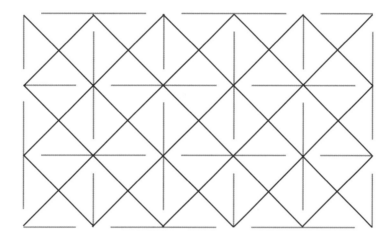

3/4" Horizontal/Vertical Grid

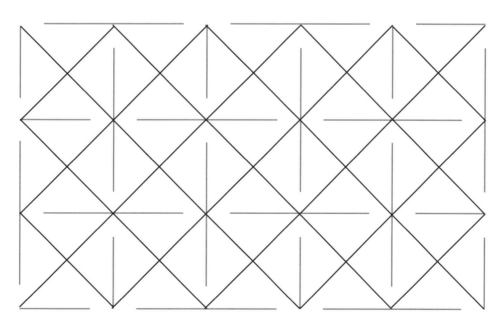

1" Horizontal/Vertical Grid

Chapter 11:
Pinwheels

The Pinwheel design is most commonly seen in patchwork, but it makes a striking design in our quilting as well. When used in borders or sashing, it frames the central design beautifully.

This design is one of those that requires a bit of studying in order to draw it and stitch it correctly. The key to mastering this design is to remember that instead of thinking in terms of a single block in your grid, you must think of four blocks in your grid.

Don't think of your grid like this:

Think of it like this:

Before getting started, there is one very important thing you must remember to make this stitch successful. The area that you're going to place it in must be divisible by two of whatever size grid you're using.

Examples: Your sashing strips are 2" wide by 8" long.

You can use either a 1" grid or a ½" grid successfully for this size of sashing. You cannot use a ¾" grid because 2 isn't evenly divisible by .75, and neither is 8.

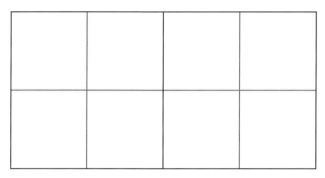

1" Grid

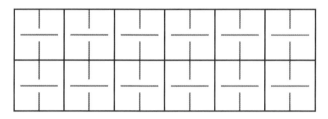

½" Grid

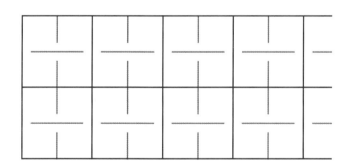

¾" Grid

However, a ¾" grid WILL WORK for sashing or borders that are evenly divisible by 1½ (2 x grid size).

For instance, a 1½" x 7½" sashing, or a 3" x 27" border

Procedure:

1. Mark your horizontal/vertical grid first.

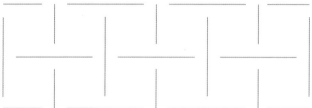

With a ruler, mark an "X" (two diagonal lines) through four of the individual blocks in your grid.

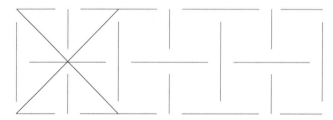

Repeat marking "X"s through each set of 4 blocks in your grid.

Note: Look at how a complete set of 4 small grid blocks fits perfectly into this corner (photo above). That's why the size of your area (sashing, border, etc.,) must be evenly divisible by two times the size of your grid.

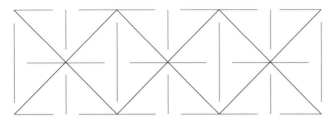

2. Once your entire grid is marked, you must stitch all of these lines. You may use your walking foot, free-motion technique, or ruler and ruler foot. I prefer to use my ¼" ruler and ruler foot. Be sure to quilt the horizontal and vertical lines first. (This portion of the stitch is not a "continuous" exercise, unless you have matching thread and employ a lot of backtracking.)

3. When you are ready to start filling in the triangles of your Pinwheels, it is helpful to mark the triangles ahead of time that need to be filled in. I simply put an "X" in each of those triangles with a wash-away marker.

4. Now that you've finished all the prep work for this design, it's time for the fun and easy part: filling in the triangles.

Quilt this design in rows so that it is continuous.

When you finish one row of X triangles, travel over to the next row and stitch back in the opposite direction until all X triangles are filled.

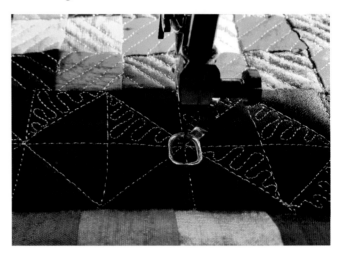

Note: If you quilt the incorrect triangle, you MUST STOP and remove those stitches because there's no covering up mistakes in this design. One wrongly quilted triangle will throw off your entire Pinwheel design.

Notice in this photo where the stitched Pinwheels were done incorrectly. It looks like a Flying Geese block instead of a Pinwheel block. That mistake had to be removed because it threw off the entire design for the rest of the border.

Photos of two quilts with Pinwheels in the border using colored thread

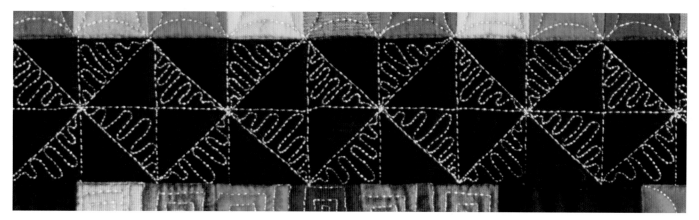

The purple border has a Pinwheel quilting design with a colored thread. The black outer border has a Pinwheel design quilted with gold metallic thread.

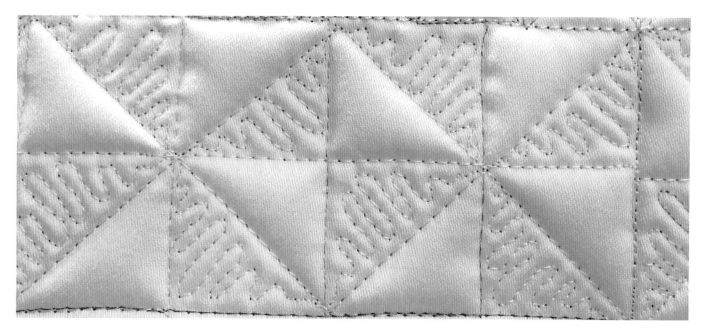

Notice that when a matching thread is used for the Pinwheel design, you see the "puff" of the design much more than the thread.

Filling in the triangles

Start

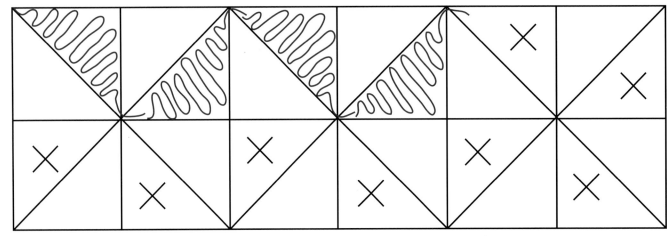

Stitch one row at a time, traveling at corners of the "X" triangles to make stitching continuous.

Chapter 12:
Twisted Ginkgos

I wonder if you'll agree with me when I say that I've saved the best design for last. The Twisted Ginkgo design is my all-time favorite grid-based quilting design.

The first time I ever saw this type of quilting was in one of Diane Gaudynski's quilts. I was amazed by its beauty, and the fact that I couldn't figure out how it was quilted. Isn't that something that we quilters appreciate? When your jaw drops at something beautiful and you wonder how in the world she (or he) quilted that!

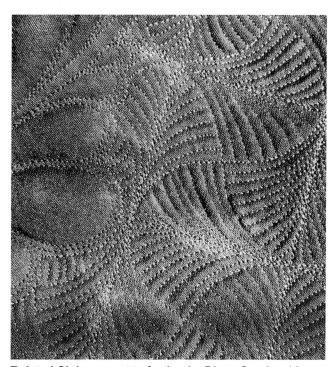

Twisted Ginkgos next to feather by Diane Gaudynski

Denim clutch purse by Diane Gaudynski

Later on in a class with Cindy Needham, I learned how Cindy came up with a simple way to mark the grid for this design, and she has graciously granted me permission to share her "twisted clam" grid and quilting technique.

Procedure:

Before we get started, please refer to the diagram below so that you will know what I'm talking about when I say "the Ginkgo tip" or "the top of the Ginkgo leaf." This design is quilted "tip to top to tip," so you should be familiar with the terms.

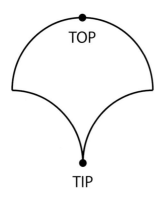

There are two ways of marking the grid for this design, so I'll cover them both and you can decide which method you prefer.

Method #1 (Cindy Needham's method)

1. Mark your grid on the diagonal with your wash-away marker. (This will NOT be stitched.) With your marker, draw an arc from the top point of one of the grid squares to the bottom point of that same square. In the next square, draw another arc, but in the opposite direction. Continue to mark the arcs in each square all the way down your grid, repeating that "S" curve. Then skip over one row of squares and mark that line EXACTLY like the first row. Every other row in your grid will be filled with "S" curves and all of them will be exactly parallel.

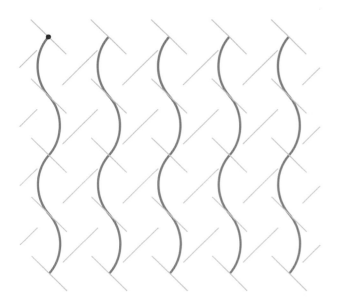

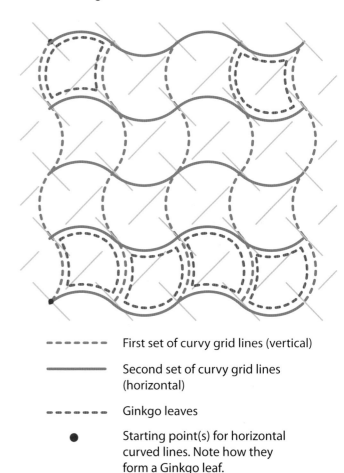

Note the spacing of the vertical curved lines (A row of grid squares is skipped.) All curved lines are parallel. Mark the first set of curved lines on the diagonal grid.

2. After completing the vertical lines, add the horizontal lines. Make sure that all these lines are parallel to each other. Be sure to start the horizontal curvy line at either the TIP of the Ginkgo leaf or at the TOP of the leaf (to form a leaf). If you don't do this, your curvy grid will not look like Ginkgo leaves.

- - - - -	First set of curvy grid lines (vertical)
———	Second set of curvy grid lines (horizontal)
- - - - -	Ginkgo leaves
●	Starting point(s) for horizontal curved lines. Note how they form a Ginkgo leaf.

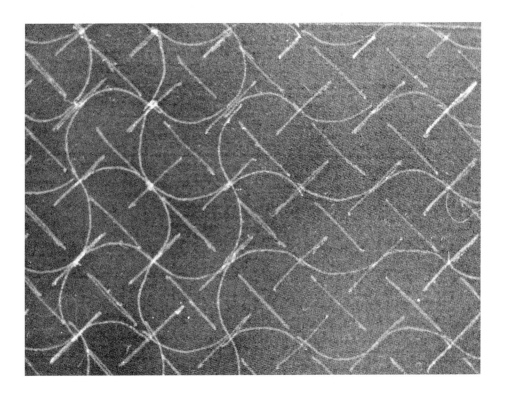

3. Once you have completely marked your curvy grid to form the Ginkgos, free motion stitch the curvy grid with the same thread that you'll be using to quilt your entire design.

4. Fill in the Ginkgo leaves.

A) Start at the tip of a Ginkgo leaf and quilt one half of the leaf (arrows show direction of stitching). Be sure you don't cross over the marked center line.

B) Once that half of the leaf is filled in, you will be at the top of the leaf. From there, stitch down the marked center line* to the TIP of the leaf.

C) Stitch the other half of the Ginkgo leaf just like you did in step 1.

D) Once you've filled in the second half of the leaf, you'll be at the top of the leaf again, and that will put you at the TIP of the adjoining leaf.

E) Repeat steps 1-4 in the adjoining leaf.

NOTE: You may also "pre-quilt" the center lines of the leaves if you wish. It's an added step, but in the end it makes the center of the leaf more precise.

Stitching the left half of the Ginkgo leaf (Note how I've stopped at the center line each time.)

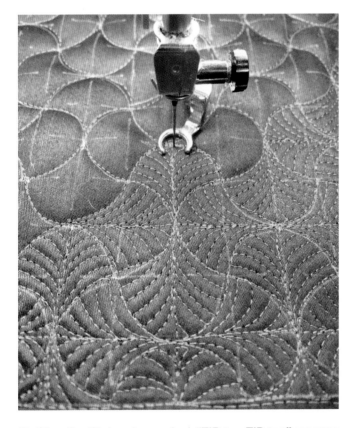

Quilting the Ginkgo leaves in a "TIP-top-TIP-top" manner (Notice how I'm finished with the current leaf at its top, and ready to start the adjoining leaf at its TIP.)

Method #2

This method is easier in some ways because it's not quite as confusing as marking your grid on the diagonal, however there is one extra step involved which adds a bit more time.

1. Mark your grid on the horizontal/vertical axis with your wash-away pen. (Note: I suggest NOT using a ½" grid for this method because the Ginkgos end up very small). Once you have your horizontal and vertical lines drawn, draw your curvy grid from the intersection in one square to the next intersection. An easy way to see how this curvy grid is drawn is to think back to our earlier chapter when we learned to quilt the Cathedral Windows design. Marking this curvy grid is simply like quilting one-half of the Cathedral Windows pattern. Mark all vertical lines with this half Cathedral Windows, soft "S" pattern. Draw your curvy grid exactly the same on all of the vertical lines in your quilting space. All lines should be parallel and look identical.

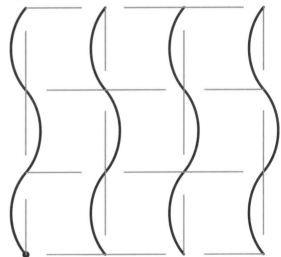

2. Once you have all of your vertical lines completed, follow the same procedure for the horizontal curvy grid lines. Remember to start the horizontal curvy grid in the proper direction (i.e., so that the curves form a Ginkgo leaf).

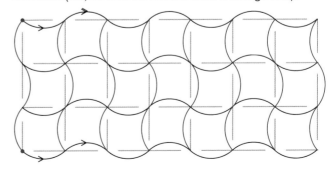

Correct starting point for horizontal curvy grid

3. Once you have all of your horizontal and vertical curvy grid lines marked, use your ruler and draw a diagonal line through the centers of the Ginkgo leaves. Now you have a stopping point for the first half of the Ginkgo leaf.

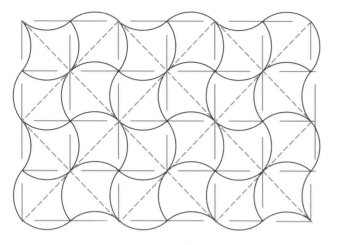

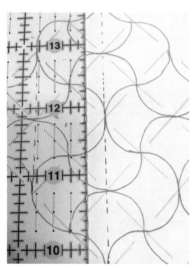

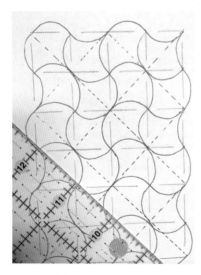

Adding the lines with a ruler to mark the center of the Ginkgo leaf

4. When the curvy grid is completely marked, stitch the curvy grid lines first, then fill in the Ginkgo leaves the same way as in Method 1.

The following examples are Twisted Ginkgos in various colors, sizes, and grid orientation.

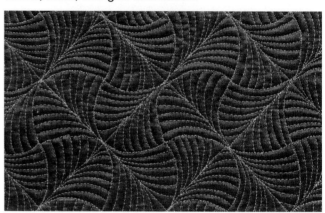

Green silk fabric with gold silk thread

Grid marked on the diagonal

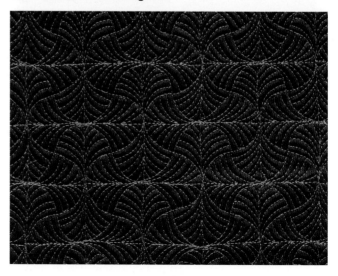

Grid marked horizontal/vertical

TIP
When looking at the following diagrams, note the size difference of the Ginkgos depending on how the grid is marked.

Actual sizes of Twisted Ginkgos:

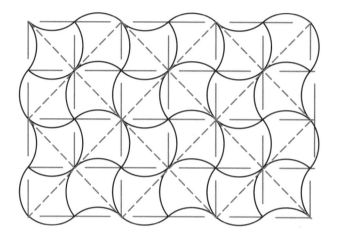

½" Horizontal/Vertical Grid

½" Diagonal Grid

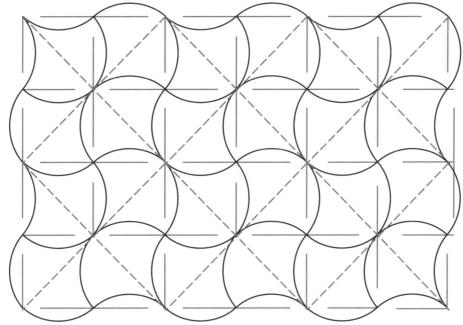

¾" Horizontal/Vertical Grid

¾" Diagonal Grid

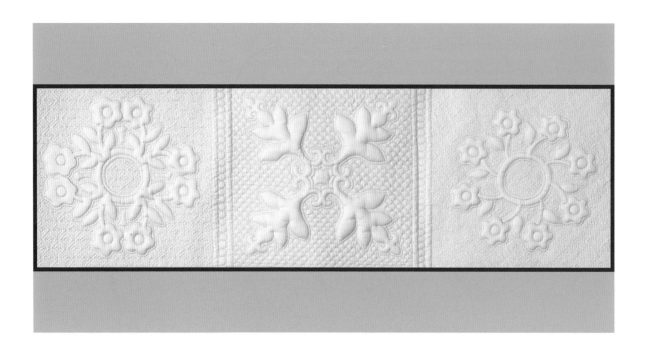

Chapter 13:
Washing and Blocking

Congratulations on finishing your quilt! At this point, you're just a few steps away from completing your masterpiece.

The grid-based quilting designs covered in this book usually fill your quilt very densely and therefore can cause some distortion. I strongly advise that you block your quilt in order to make it hang or lie flat and square.

The first thing that needs to be done is to remove all quilting marks. This is my procedure:

1. To remove blue wash-away marks, I fill my washing machine with cold, clear water (i.e., no soaps, detergents, etc., because you never know which chemicals might react with the blue wash-away ink). Then I put the quilt into the cold water and manually agitate it so that all parts of it get wet. If you don't agitate your quilt enough, there could be little hidden nooks and crannies that don't get wet, and that can be a problem. You want the quilt completely wet so that all the blue marks dissipate.

2. Once I am certain that the entire quilt is soaked, I then set the washing machine to spin so that all the water in the machine drains out, and most of the water in the quilt is spun out, too.

3. At this point, if I also have quilting marks from a white iron-away pen, I will refill the washing machine with warm water to remove the white marks. Be careful though, because if you have fabrics that tend to bleed, the warm water will cause more fabric bleeding to occur. Once your washer is filled with warm water, repeat the process of hand agitating your quilt to make sure all areas are completely submerged in warm water. When done, set the washer on spin to remove as much water as possible from the quilt.

Supplies for The Blocking Process:
Large, flat sheet
Strong straight pins
Long ruler or yardstick
Yarn (or a laser level tool if you have one)
Oscillating fan
Tape measure

The next step in blocking my quilts is to lay out a clean sheet on a carpeted floor. The sheet must be a little bigger than the quilt. Take the wet quilt out of the washing machine and lay it out on the sheet. Smooth out the entire surface of the quilt and begin to visually make sure it's starting to "square up."

The next thing I do is measure the sides of the quilt. If it's a square quilt, all sides should be equal. If you find that one side is shorter than the others, use your hands to spread out the wet quilt even more, thereby lengthening that shorter side. If your quilt is rectangular, the two sides will be equal, and the top and bottom will also be equal to each other. Again, if you need to smooth out the wet quilt a bit more to make the sides equal, do this now.

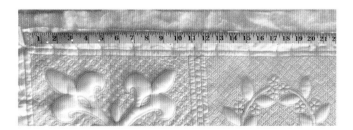

Once my sides are equal, I pin the top edge of the quilt about every 2"–3" with the straight pins. This is when I use my yarn and pins to make a "plumb" line so that the top edge is straight.

Once I get that top edge securely pinned, I start working on the opposite (bottom) edge of the quilt. Before pinning the bottom edge, I use my yarn (plumb line) or laser level to make sure the corners are square and perpendicular to the top edge. As you pin the bottom edge, make sure it's straight.

After pinning the top and bottom edges of the quilt, I work on the two sides. Again I use my yarn (plumb line) to make sure those edges are straight and the corners are square.

Cindy's yarn plumb line

Yarn plumb line along the side of the quilt to use as a guide to get edge of quilt straight

NOTE: Since I have not trimmed the excess batting and backing from my quilt, it will be visible at all times. I just ignore that and focus on the quilt top. That's what we want to "square up."

When all four sides of the quilt are pinned and appear straight and even, it's time to look at the inside of the quilt, i.e., borders, sashing, rows of blocks, etc. To me there's nothing more obvious in a quilt than when a straight line isn't straight. So now is the time to make those straight lines behave and straighten up! Again, I use the yarn (or laser level) and nudge those borders into a straight line and hold them there with pins. I don't worry about how many pins I use. I just use as many as it takes to do the job.

Yarn plumb line used on inner sashing as a guide for straightening that sashing

When at long last I stand back and look at the quilt with a very critical eye and feel satisfied that everything is where I want it to be (edges, borders, seam lines), I set up my oscillating fan so that it covers the entire surface of the quilt. Then I leave the quilt under the fan for 24 hours. I also turn on the ceiling fan to add extra drying power.

After the 24-hour drying period is up, I remove all of the straight pins and take the quilt back to my sewing room to trim the excess batting and backing from the quilt.

Binding Your Quilt

The last step for me is to bind the quilt. The reason I do this last is because if I attach the binding after washing and blocking the quilt, it doesn't get that puckered look that binding can get once a quilt is washed (however, note that I have prewashed the binding fabric).

> ### TIP
> Other options for blocking your quilt on your carpet: Foam insulation boards (can be purchased at home improvement stores), or a cardboard fold-out cutting board

Grid Designs

If you're reading this portion of the book, that can mean only one thing: you have completed reading the entire book! I am so happy you persevered. I know that these grid-based designs require a lot of work and practice, but I'm sure you now realize just how much they can enhance your quilts.

Once your eyes are opened to grid-based designs, you'll start to see them wherever you go. If you're like me, when you see them, you'll be inspired to figure out how to quilt them and which of your quilts you can use them in. So have fun and create something beautiful!

A SPLENDID DISPLAY by Cindy Seitz-Krug

Twisted Ginkgos in blue silk thread as a background for a quilting motif

DELECTABLE MOUNTAINS by Diane Gaudynski

Orange Peel and Twisted Ginkgos in dark brown triangles

Clamshell variation in dark brown triangles

SIMPLY SANTA FE by Cindy Seitz-Krug

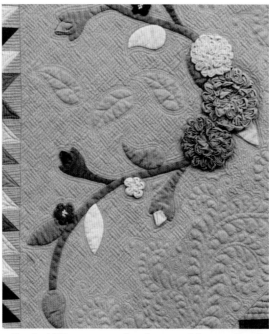

Basket Weave as a background for appliqué

LINDA'S FOLLY BY Cindy Seitz-Krug

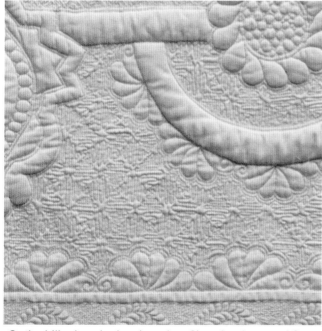

Optical Illusion design (number 2) as background for feather motifs

Basket Weave design as background for feather motif

RABBIT IN GREEN by Diane Gaudynski

Orange Peel design in outer border

Clamshells in outer edge of green silk

EVERLASTING BOUQUET by Molly Hamilton-McNally and Cindy Seitz-Krug

Orange Peel design as a background for feather motif

LIFE IS FRAGILE...HANDLE WITH PRAYER by Cindy Needham

Clamshells design as background for elaborate quilting motif

ODE TO SPRING by Margaret Solomon Gunn

Ginkgo Clamshells as a beautiful background

SHADOWS OF UMBRIA by Diane Gaudynski

Orange Peel design used on outer border

My Brunette Whig by Gail Stepanek and Jan Hutchison

Detail of setting squares showing Checkerboard quilting design

MOLLY & ME, appliquéd and quilted by Cindy Seitz-Krug. Appliqué pattern by Molly Hamilton-McNally.

Cathedral Window design as a background to the appliqué

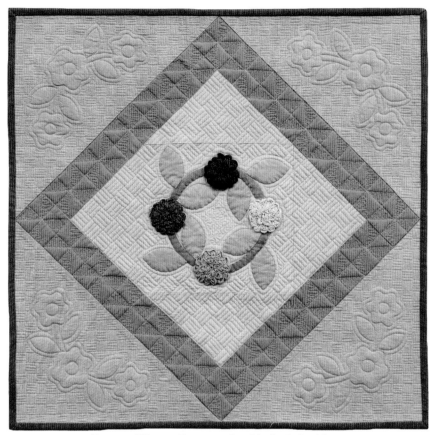

BASKET WEAVE SAMPLER by Cindy Seitz-Krug

CLAMSHELL SAMPLER by Cindy Seitz-Krug

PLOVER SAMPLER by Cindy Seitz-Krug

SQUARE IN A SQUARE SAMPLER by Cindy Seitz-Krug

OPTICAL ILLUSION SAMPLER by Cindy Seitz-Krug

DOUBLE/TRIPLE GRID by Cindy Seitz-Krug

Practice Pages

Do you remember when you were in elementary school, learning to print and then writing in cursive? I doubt if there's a person on this earth who doesn't remember those pages of letters and words that we had to practice for hours on end. But that's how we learned to print and handwrite. It was quite an effective teaching method! So, I thought that if you have trouble remembering how to quilt the grid-based designs in this book, these practice sheets would serve to remind you, or get your brain warmed up to the "flow" of the designs.

Clamshell

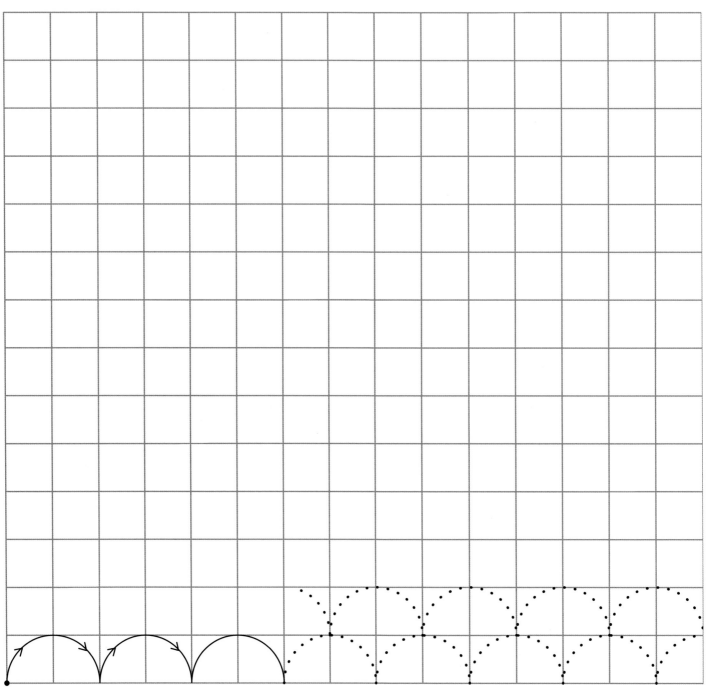

Start at bottom and work upward

Cathedral Windows & Orange Peel

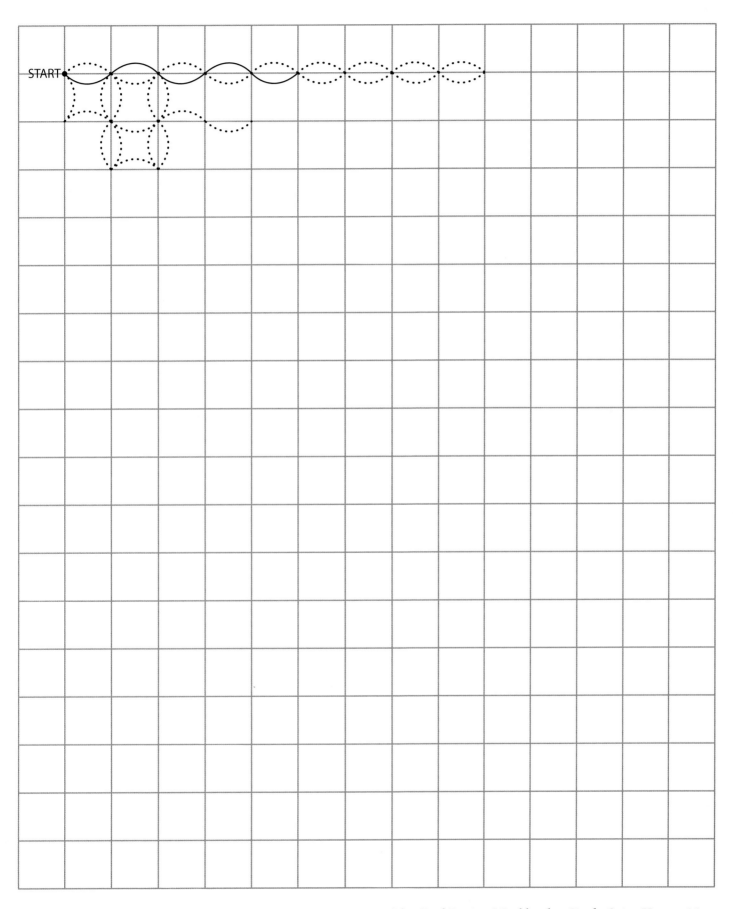

Basket Weave

START

Optical Illusion

Checkerboard

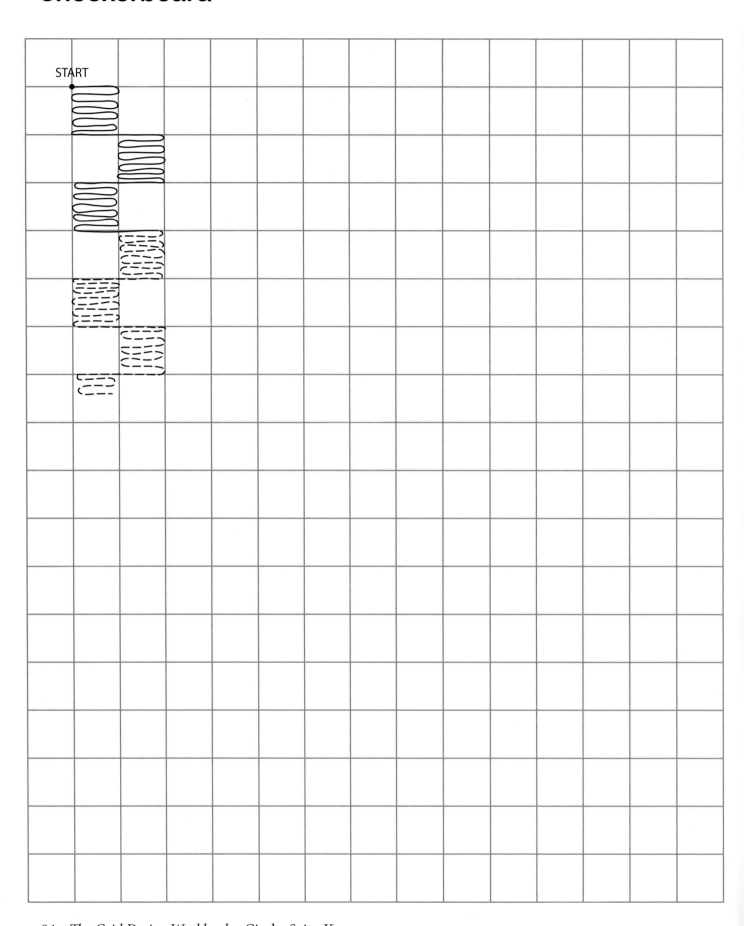

START

Square in a Square

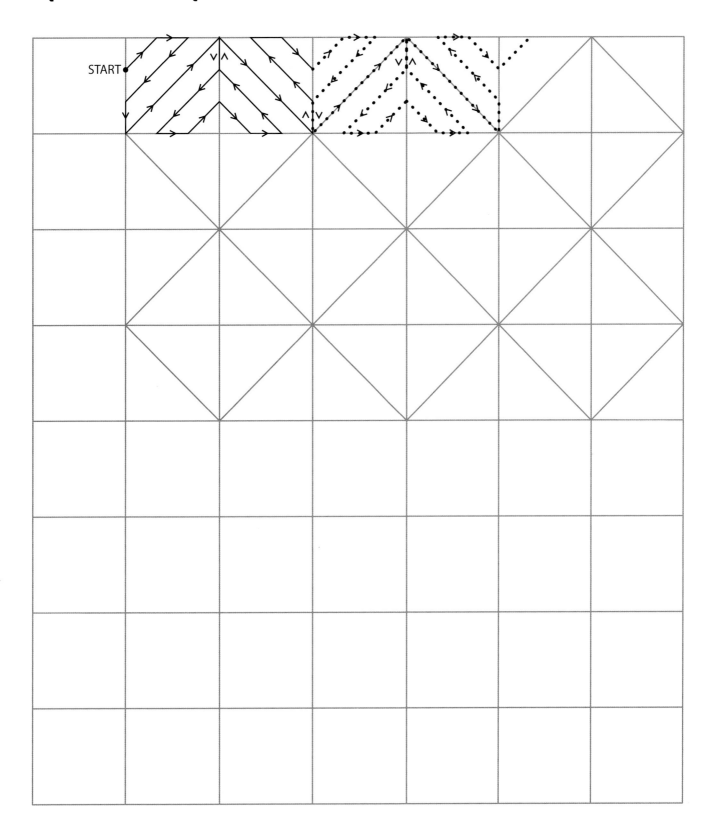

START

Greek Key

START

Plover

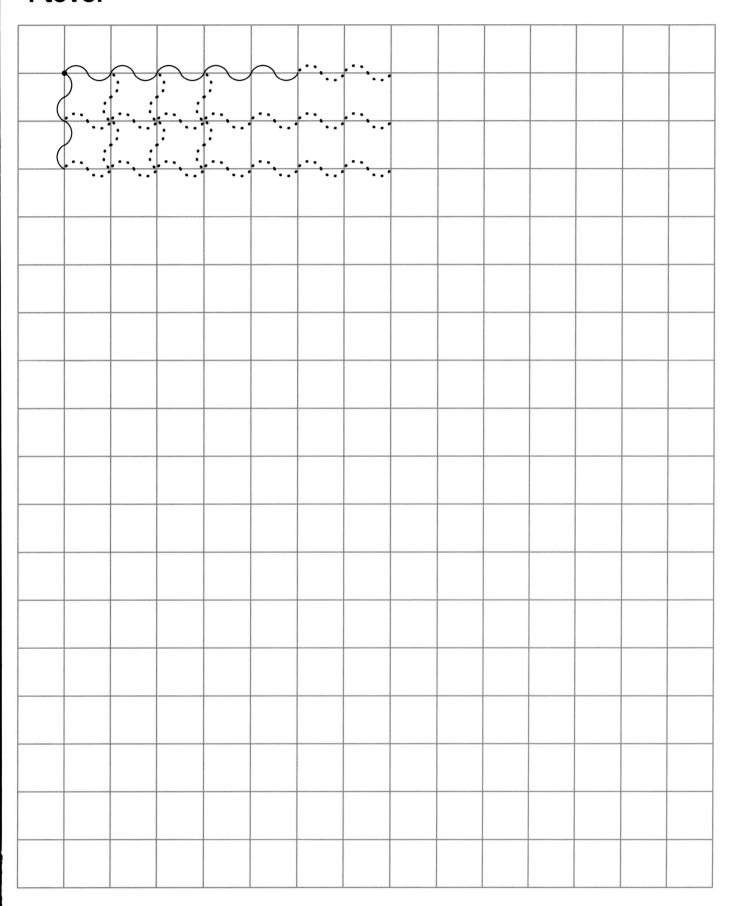

Pinwheels

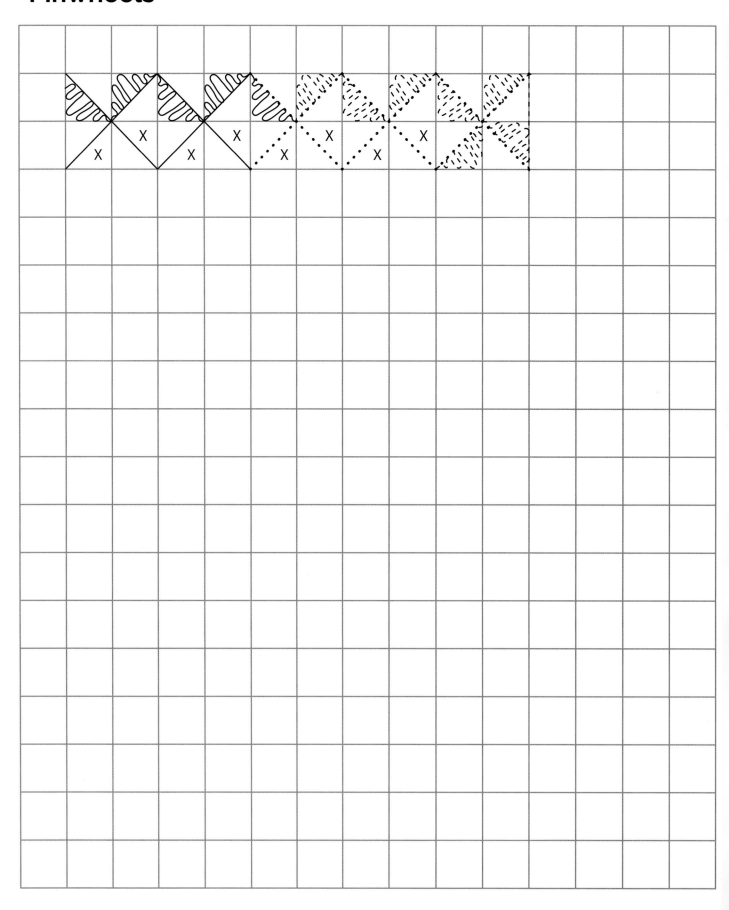

Twisted Ginkgos

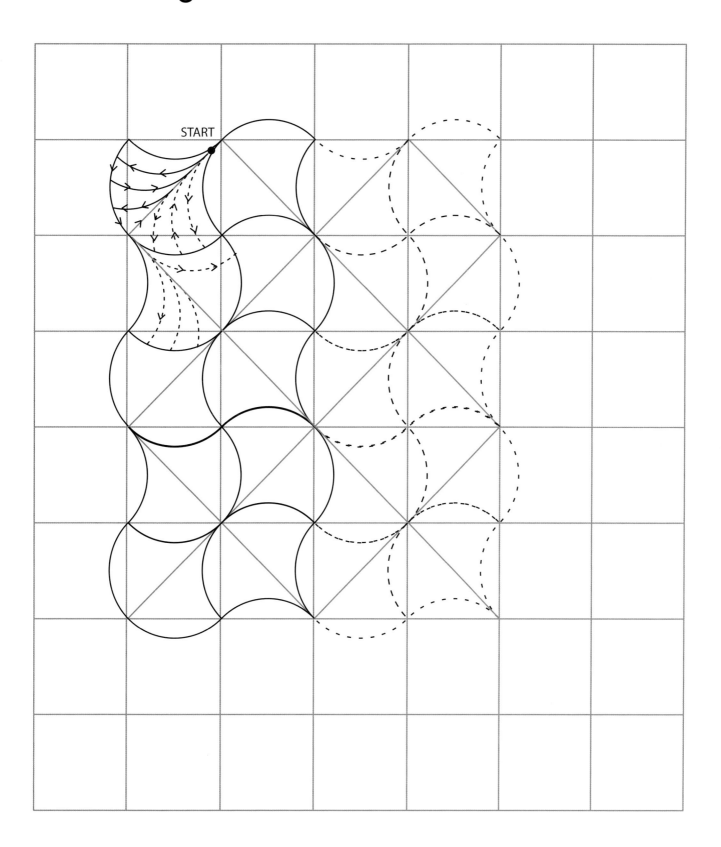

START

¼" Grid (Horizontal/Vertical)

¼" Grid (Diagonal)

½" Grid (Horizontal/Vertical)

½" Grid (Diagonal)

GORGEOUS GRIDDED QUILTING DESIGNS SAMPLER QUILT by Cindy Seitz-Krug

About the Author

I was born and raised in Ventura, California. Since a very early age I loved working on arts and crafts. My grandmother taught me to crochet when I was around six years old, and by the time I was seven I was crocheting shawls for all of the neighbor ladies. As with most people who enjoy arts and crafts, I ran the gamut—from beading to needlepoint to crochet, and so on. When I was 28 years old I finally arrived at quilting. From the very first quilt I made, I was hooked! In the 24 years that I've been quilting, I don't think I've ever gone back to any of those other crafts. Quilting has become an integral part of me.

I've always gravitated toward making traditional quilts, but I really love innovative quilts which take traditional patterns and enhance them. After quilting for only about five or six years, I started entering my quilts in small regional shows. I've always loved to share my work. What I soon learned was that I really enjoyed competing in quilt competitions. When I earned a "Best of Show" award at my first "large" regional quilt show that I entered, I started to really focus on good workmanship and design. But what I really became known for was my machine quilting.

My quilting tends to be very structured and symmetrical. I just love the look of elegant, heirloom-style quilting. I don't think that kind of beauty can ever go out of style. In this day of "fast and furious" and "instant gratification," I still believe that spending extra time and effort on your quilts pays off exponentially. I always tell my students that they'll never regret the extra time spent in quilting their quilts. They may moan and groan about having to do some additional quilting before diving in to the project, but they won't regret it afterwards. In fact, they'll be very happy they put in that extra effort.

One of the reasons that I wrote this book is I felt that the pendulum was swinging away from quilters being in such a hurry to finish quilts, and was swinging toward quilters taking extra time to create even more lovely quilts. Grid-based quilting designs do take extra time, but the result never fails to impress people. I'm hoping that this book will take some of the mystery out of how those designs are achieved.

Besides quilting, I love spending time in the mountains with my husband and our grown son and daughter. We enjoy hunting and fishing in the Rocky Mountains. I have a Bachelor's degree in environmental and systematic biology, with a concentration in fisheries. For twenty five years my husband and I owned several aquaculture farms in California, but these days we reside in the beautiful White Mountains of Arizona.

Enjoy these and more from AQS

AQS Publishing brings the latest in quilt topics to satisfy the traditional to modern quilter. Interesting techniques, vivid color, and clear directions make these books your one-stop for quilt design and instruction. With its leading Quilt-Fiction series, mystery, relationship, and community all merge as stories are pieced together to keep you spell-bound.

Whether Quilt-Instruction or Quilt-Fiction, pick one up from AQS today.

12518

12512

12520

10274

12524

12514

12516

12510

12522

AQS publications are available nationwide.
Call or visit AQS

www.shopAQS.com
1-800-626-5420